seems to get more complicated, Col-
ome-spun simplicity coupled with
als for professional sales success.
we need to dummy down and get

— Brian Hamilton
Principal
Land Title Guarantee Company

high performing sales team means
ith the right trainer, Colleen Stanley.
d our sales culture and improved pro-
by adhering to the values shared in

— Michele Dressel
President
Alpine Bank Mortgage

As a forme
from the co
freshing. The
agers to buil

Co-author of

In a world that
leen provides
the fundament
Let's face it . . .
back to work.

Your straight f
business is terr
plishing goals b
job done. It's rea
the lessons descri

Developing a
partnering w
We've change
fessionalism
this book.

Thank you! Finally,
on "real world" expe
clichés. This is powe
the real world.

V

Growing Great Sales Teams

Lessons from the Cornfield

By Colleen Stanley

Heartland Press

Growing Great Sales Teams

Lessons from the Cornfield

Published by:
Heartland Press, Inc.
149 Willowleaf Dr.
Littleton, CO 80127 U. S. A.

Names in some stories have been changed
to protect identities of persons involved.

ISBN - 0-9778375-0-5

Printed in Canada.
First printing in May, 2006

Jacket design and interior by Karen Saunders, MacGraphics Services
Jacket photo by Jim Rae
Illustration © 2006 Joyce M Turley, Dixon Cove Design

Library of Congress Cataloging-in-Publication Data
Stanley, Colleen Stanley
Growing Great Sales Teams: Lessons from the Cornfield

1. Sales & Selling 2. Management 3. Leadership

I. Stanley, Colleen. I. Title

Dedication

To my parents, Bill and Monica Schany. Thanks for not believing the doctors.

To my big sister, Anne Marie Nelson. You are a great example of "walking the talk."

To my husband, Jim Stanley, my rock and best friend. Your unconditional support always amazes me.

Acknowledgements

I believe it's important to remember where you came from and who helped get you where you are today. I'm fortunate because I've been blessed with great teachers, mentors, and friends who have encouraged and supported me.

Thanks to the management team at Varsity Spirit Corporation—Don Trandem, Kline Boyd, Jeff Webb, Bob Dunseath and John Nichols. You gave me an opportunity in sales and sales management without any prior experience. Thanks for taking the "leap of faith."

To my assistant, Dawn Riedmann, thank you. You do a great job of working "behind the scenes" so I can be on the scene. And you do it with a wonderful sense of humor and good attitude.

Jill Scott, my editor. Thank you for your eagle eye and honesty. You were adamant about copy not going to print unless it made sense and made a contribution.

Thank you dear friends, of which there are too many to name. Your timing is always impeccable with words of support and advice.

To the good people of Iowa. Don't quit teaching the lessons of the cornfield. They are timeless principles that need to be shared.

Table of Contents

Introduction

My first lessons in business were not taught around a conference table or in a strategy meeting. I learned them in wide-open spaces, cornfields, and barnyards. My teachers were my parents, siblings, and community members. It is in Iowa where I learned "heartland principles" for success in business—honesty, hard work, risk taking, fairness with business partners, and staying grounded.

The most important principle? Staying grounded while achieving success. People of the heartland manage to remain authentic in a name-dropping society. They do not fall in love with their own "press," but do practice the golden rule of treating others the way they want to be treated, regardless of title or status.

I hope this book serves as a reminder that in this high-tech, competitive world, common sense business principles still prevail. We can receive information 24/7 and create global companies overnight, but at the end of the day, it is still the principles of the heartland that create great companies and sales organizations.

I moved from the cornfields of Iowa into the corporate boardroom by taking a sales position with a small start-up company, Varsity Spirit Corporation. This company built itself on the same good values I learned growing up on an Iowa farm. They gave people without business experience an opportunity to succeed because they showed up and tried. They believed in building relationships and took risks that eventually made them the number one company in their industry. During my ten years at Varsity Spirit Corporation, we grew from $8 million in revenues to $90 million. It was quite a ride and one that I am grateful to have purchased a ticket.

So go grab a cup of coffee, take a minute to slow down, and read about heartland principles for building high-performance sales teams.

Lesson 1

Staying Grounded on the Road to Success

People from Iowa are described as friendly, genuine, and authentic. In other words, they are very grounded. Name dropping or posturing doesn't work well in Iowa because Iowans don't dwell on the name you drop or the posture you assume. The car you drive or the labels you wear just aren't important in day-to-day life. An old high school friend reminded me of this important heartland principle many years later in my corporate career.

When I resigned from Varsity Spirit Corporation, the company generously gave me a Rolex watch as a "retirement" gift. I appreciated my new expensive watch and was dying to call someone and "name drop" my new piece of jewelry. I was feeling like a bit of a big shot and a long way from being grounded!

I called my friend, Diane, who still lives in Iowa, and mentioned my expensive "going-away" gift. Diane, always a great supporter, shared in my excitement by yelling to her husband, "Joe, you are not going to believe what Varsity gave Colleen as a going away gift. They gave her a rolodex." Yes, you are reading the sentence correctly. *A rolodex.* (Remember, name dropping doesn't mean anything in Iowa.) When your ego is starting to inflate, people from the heartland immediately figure out a way to bring you back to Earth, back to being grounded.

How to Keep Your Sales Team Grounded While Elevating Sales

Strong sales organizations are grounded. They never catch the disease of business arrogance, which lowers immunity and increases susceptibility to another disease: complacency. The irony of this disease is that the very things that create successful organizations (where they have the choice of becoming arrogant or remaining grounded) are the very things that go away after contracting the disease.

Case in point: A motivated, new salesperson is eager to learn new ideas and concepts that will help him/her succeed in the business. He attends seminars, asks for advice, practices and continues to increase his intellect and skills. On the other hand, the successful, veteran salesperson can become complacent, believing that she has learned everything necessary to succeed. Business acumen and skills slowly start to decline and mediocre habits creep in.

I remember hearing a fellow sales trainer speak at a national conference. This gentleman was a ten-year veteran in the business and openly shared that his business had decreased over the last year. The decrease wasn't due to the economy; it was caused by his not practicing what he preached in his sales training courses, not executing the fundamentals, and learning new skills necessary to succeed in a changing business environment. He reminded all the sales gurus sitting in the audience that it didn't matter how much we knew about sales, it only mattered how much we were willing to continue learning and changing.

So how do you keep your sales team grounded on their journey to the top? Continually remind them that the practices and attitudes that propelled you to the top cannot be forgotten as they grow more successful. Learning, growing, and being open to change are deterrents to arrogance and complacency.

Challenge your team and test for the disease of arrogance and complacency by asking the following questions:

1. Are we smarter than we were two weeks ago? How and where?

2. What did you do this week to improve as a sales professional?

3. If you were a prospect, would you select *you* over the competition?

4. When is the last time you have done something outside your comfort zone?

Accu Bite Dental Supply is a company representing one of America's great success stories. They were named an "Inc. 500 Company" and one of the fastest growing, privately held companies.

As a guest speaker at their national sales meeting, I listened to Dr. William Costello, CEO, chairman, and founder of Accu Bite. Dr. Costello shared with the sales team that he was often asked what the key was to his success. Here is what he told the group: "Every morning when I get up, I look in the mirror and say, I can do better." It is obvious that Dr. Costello has never caught the disease of arrogance and is intent on instilling a grounded mentality in his organization.

Grounded sales teams will always outperform the arrogant sales team because they are smarter, open to change, and hungry to win. Remember, the only time you can afford not to change, grow, or improve is when your competitor has made the same decision.

Lesson 2

Harvest and Sales: Get the Sales Crop In

Farmers don't use terms such as "hitting sales goals" or "achieving quota." Rather, they speak about "getting the crops in."

During the fall, every farm family is working under a deadline of getting the crops in before snow falls. My parents worked 24/7 during this time of the year. In looking back on that time, I am amazed that after working many long days to get their crops in, my parents would not kick back and take well-deserved time off. Instead, they checked in with their neighbors and volunteered to help them get their crops in if they were running behind. There was no conversation about payback for the wear and tear on equipment or time used to help a fellow neighbor reap his harvest. They felt that it was important to help their neighbors reach their "sales goal."

In the good 'ole days, farmers were well-disguised, strategic management consultants. They saw the 50,000-foot view and understood if every farmer got his crop in—hit his sales goal—there would be more money to contribute to businesses, schools, recreation, and churches. They knew if each farmer hit their goal, the whole team would win.

As a new salesperson with Varsity, I was fortunate to work with sales professionals who had a farmer's mentality. I was the new kid on the block and didn't know anything about sales or customer service. The company was young and didn't have the personnel or money to train new hires.

Lucky for me, Varsity recruited four veterans to their team. Patty and Gary Stuart, Lynette White, and Betty Black were farmers in disguise. I took turns calling (OK, *pestering*) the veterans asking for advice on products, tough customers, or just plain old sales. They always offered their time and advice without hesitation. They received no commission override on my sales or recognition for my success; however, Patty, Gary, Betty, and Lynette saw the big picture. They knew if every salesperson on the Varsity team "got their crops in" the company would thrive and grow. They were correct and Varsity became the number one player in the industry, eventually becoming a public company.

Creating a "Sales Farming Culture"

What would happen if your sales team adopted the old-fashioned farm mentality and developed a true concern for their fellow salesperson getting their "sales crop" in? What would happen if your star salesperson—who is hitting their quota early in the year—took a day or two to help a fellow team member who is new or in a slump hit their own sales goal? Maybe, just maybe, more sales organizations would reap a bountiful harvest.

Create a farming mentality:

1. **Recruit people who are givers and not takers.**
   Salespeople with a farmer's mentality possess that wonderful abundance attitude. They want each person on the sales team to be very good. They share knowledge and strategies because they realize a sales team of excellence is a force to be reckoned with in the market place. This type of person remembers being a rookie, hitting a slump, and knows that someone mentored or helped them along the way.

2. **Take time to share best practices during sales meetings.**
   There is a lot of brilliance on every sales team. One salesperson is extraordinary in customer retention; another is highly skilled in customer acquisition. The problem is that most organizations don't have a structure or system to share this talent, and best practices are rarely duplicated.

3. **Create mentor programs.**
   Most successful business people belong to a "mas-

ter mind" group. These groups keep members accountable to goals and continually work to raise the sales bar. Create a master mind group within your own sales organization or encourage your team to become part of a master mind. Mom was right when she said, "Tell me who your friends are, and I will tell what you are like." Winners hang around winners and those mired in mediocrity hang around their own kind.

Get your sales team farming. The world is too competitive not to help fellow team members get their "sales crop in."

Lesson 3

Take Risks: Show Up and Try

If you were to play a word association game, you probably would not associate the words "risk taking" with Iowa. People usually associate words such as corn, beans, cows, or pigs. Contrary to perception, growing up in Iowa is a great place to learn how to take risks. In Iowa, however, it is not called risk taking: it's called showing up and trying.

I learned this lesson well from my years on the West Bend Community High School dance team. Jan Gruber, our high school Spanish teacher, decided that West Bend needed a dance team. Many of my classmates had never seen a pair of dance slippers, much less a dance studio. In fact, the old term "can't walk and chew gum" probably evolved from an observer watching the first practices of our newly formed dance team. Jan Gruber didn't care about our lack of experience; she only cared that we showed up and tried. And we did, practicing for hours, learning how to work as a team.

After hours of practice, Jan decided that West Bend was ready to compete in their first dance competition. Because dance competition was in its infancy in Iowa, competing schools were not divided by class or size. Little West Bend Community High School would be competing against schools and teams four times our size. Some people might consider entering this type of competition risky. We didn't consider it a risk because we only knew one philosophy—*show up and try.*

Our first entry into competition resulted in winning first place and the showmanship award. It also resulted in my learning an important lesson:

Show up and try. Sometimes you discover a talent you never knew you had and sometimes you become excellent.

Small-town kids learn at an early age that you don't have to be good or excellent *before* attempting something new. In fact, because of the shortage of bodies, you can show up, try, and make it on the team . . . even if you're not that good! When comparing notes with friends who attended larger schools, they share the opposite philosophy. You had to be good before you even thought about auditioning for a group or sport. Unfortunately, it is at this point people learn a self-limiting belief: You have to be good before you can try a new endeavor. It is the ultimate chicken and egg scenario. (How do you ever get good at something if you never show up?)

The lesson of showing up and trying served me well in my first sales position with Varsity Spirit Corporation. Varsity is a classic David and Goliath story. Varsity was a new player in the market competing against the goliath of the industry, Cheerleader Supply, who was quadruple the size of Varsity. Cheerleader Supply had more reps, a bigger catalog, and better brand recognition. Varsity had five sales reps, a much smaller catalog, and no name recognition. Some people might view signing on with this underdog company a risky situation and a waste of time. Thank goodness, the early sales team at Varsity didn't consider it a risk because of their past schooling in "showing up and trying."

In 1994 and 1995, Varsity Spirit Corporation was named by *Forbes Magazine* as one of the 200 fastest growing companies. In 2004, Varsity Spirit Corporation acquired the goliath, Cheerleader Supply. Amazing things happen when you show up and try.

How to Create A "Show Up and Try" Sales Culture

Challenge your team and ask them why they are not showing up.

Areas of concern may be:

- The competition is bigger, therefore, the sales team perceives them to be better.

- The competition is better known, therefore, the team believes that the customer will not be responsive to meeting with a lesser-known brand.

- The team is uncomfortable approaching a new situation because it requires a different set of skills.

- The team believes they need to be perfect before they can try something new.

Then ask the most important question: How in the world do you get good at something if you don't show up and try?

A critical leadership skill in building a high-performing sales organization is teaching your team to show up and try . . . *before they are good!*

Here are a few ideas:

1. **Incorporate a "show up and try" section in your weekly/monthly sales meetings.** Encourage your sales team to share the good, the bad, and the ugly. Get your team to share stories and apply lessons learned from the stories. John Maxwell, author of *The 21 Irrefutable Laws of Leadership,* states it best: "Experience gives you

the test first and the lesson second." Teach your team to take the test and learn from mistakes.

2. **Emphasize that the successful and intelligent people in life have tried and failed more than their non-successful counterparts.**
The key is that smart people learn lessons from each failure. Do the math. If you show up and try ten times, fail ten times, learn ten lessons that will help you in the future, you are going to be *100 times smarter* than your competition. Think your team will be more open to failing after exploring that math formula?

3. **Form a "show up and try" club.**
Membership requires trying something that you aren't good at or don't think you are qualified to do. Keeping membership requires participants to try one activity per month that is uncomfortable. Reward the rep for trying the activity, regardless of results.

Show me a sales team that will show up and try and I will show you a sales organization that cannot and will not be beaten by the team that is waiting to get good before showing up.

Lesson 4

Authentic Selling: Take Yourself to the Sales Call

I had a limited sales background prior to entering the profession. Up until then, I had sold fruit (to raise money for our senior class trip), some calves in the local 4H club, and souvenirs at the Grotto of Redemption souvenir shop. I didn't know how to recognize different buying styles or ask open-ended questions. But I knew these two things: I was always enthused about what I was selling, and I knew enough to ask for the order.

This simplistic thinking served me well on my very first sales call with Varsity Spirit Corporation. I met with Otis Perry, who was the athletic director at North High School in Omaha, Nebraska. Looking back on the sales call, it could be easily labeled as pathetic. I was "spraying and praying" about the benefits of Varsity. (Spraying product knowledge and praying that Otis would buy.) I barely gave him time to breathe or ask a question. When I finally paused, Otis asked me one question: Who are you currently doing business with? That was a problem because I wasn't doing business with anyone! I bravely replied that I thought Millard South High School was going to give me an opportunity. Otis gave me his business that day and it can only be for one of two reasons: One, he felt sorry for me, or two, he realized that I was genuine, sincere, and sold on my product. Maybe it was a combination of both.

While I have become more sophisticated about selling, I am still absolutely certain that being authentic and genuine when meeting with prospects beats the slick salesperson every time.

The Authentic Salesperson

The best selling tip I give to salespeople is, "take yourself to the sales call." When I mention this as a workshop leader, at least one audience member with a furrowed brow asks, "What do you mean?"

Salespeople think they need to know everything, use heavy-handed sales techniques, and talk like a "sales doctor." They end up trying to be something they aren't and the results are painfully apparent on the call as the salesperson switches personality styles on a minute-by-minute basis. They have forgotten to be themselves, be authentic, on a sales call.

If you want to return to authenticity, take your sales team to a local playground to observe kids. Everyone loves kids because they are fresh, truthful, and authentic; they are themselves. They haven't learned how to name drop, act sophisticated, talk a certain way, or dress to please. (We are lucky if they even dress to *match*.)

As we grow into adulthood we learn a lot of "should" messages. You *should* act grown up, you *should* act like your brother, and you *shouldn't* act this way. Pretty soon, people forget about their originality, their uniqueness, and spend their whole life trying to be something they are not.

The pure delight of children and authenticity was brought to my full attention on a trip to Michigan where I was the featured sales trainer at a conference. While boarding the plane in Denver, I noticed a group of children who appeared to have some degree of intellectual handicap and at the same time were very outgoing and not afraid of strangers. They had Williams Syndrome, which is a rare genetic condition, occurring in 1 out of 20,000 births. It just so happened this group of kids were also going to Michigan, attending a conference at the same hotel as me.

Upon landing in Michigan, the kids and I boarded one of the shuttle buses to the hotel. A few minutes later, I felt a tap on my shoulder and I turned around to a toothy grin and introduction, "Hi, I am George and I am special."

I replied, "George, I have no doubt that you are!" George explained to me that he had Williams Syndrome and was missing genetic material on chromosome #7. He concluded by summarizing with, "That's what makes *me* so special."

After arriving at the hotel, I checked in and proceeded to my room. Once again, I was approached by another Williams Syndrome child attending the conference who extended her hand and said, "Hi, I am Suzie and I don't believe we have met."

I laughed and said, "No, we haven't, but I get the feeling that we are going to!"

When I got to my hotel room, I sat down to reflect on the children and my encounters with them. Initially, I had been feeling sorry for this group of kids until my interaction with them. Now, I was feeling sorry for myself! These kids had better self-esteem and were more comfortable with themselves, despite their disability, than most of the sales teams I work with. In fact, I was seriously thinking about hiring Suzie for new business development.

What would happen to your sales results if everyone on your team felt as special as George? What would happen to your sales results if everyone were as comfortable as Suzie meeting complete strangers? My guess is that there would be a lot more prospecting and closed deals.

How to Create Authenticity on Your Sales Team

As a sales manager, it is your job and responsibility to grow your team personally and professionally. Part of this equation is helping your sales team get comfortable with themselves on a sales call and appreciating their own unique style.

At your next sales meeting, pose these three questions to raise awareness on the importance of authenticity:

1. **Do people want to buy the real deal or something fake?**
   We have just gone through a time in business of dot-com bombs and corporate scandals. More than ever it is important to be real and build the foundation piece of good business: trust. If the

salesperson appears to be a fake, it poses this unasked question: What else are they faking? Their company's ability to deliver? The features of the product? Their own abilities?

2. **Where should your focus be on the call—you or the prospect?**
   Teach your team to quit worrying about what they are supposed to say and instead focus on one thing: your prospect's problem and asking questions to understand that problem. Guess what, if you are asking questions, you don't have to worry about what to say. The prospect is doing all the talking.

3. **If you aren't comfortable with who you are, why would a prospect be comfortable meeting with you?**
   Ever watch a speaker who is uncomfortable on stage? They may have a great message, however, everyone in the audience senses the nervousness and misses the message. When you are comfortable, your prospect is comfortable and willing to share more information.

Build a high performance sales team by recruiting kids or getting your sales team to act like them! Authenticity beats slick every time.

Lesson 5

Don't Lie to the Nuns—or Your Customers

I was raised in a large, Irish Catholic family with seven siblings and attended Catholic grade school for eight years. Between the Ten Commandments and confession, one would think that a child wouldn't need to learn any lessons on telling the truth or being honest. Unfortunately, I am either thick or stubborn and learned truth telling the hard way.

West Bend, Iowa, was host to many retired nuns who spent their golden years at the convent volunteering at the local grade school. I was in fourth grade when I decided to tell a big fib to one of the newly retired sisters. When she asked about my family, I proceeded to fabricate a huge story of how my parents were missionaries abroad, serving the Lord. The elderly sister was fascinated by the story and shared it with the other sisters at dinner that evening.

The next day I was hauled into the principal's office. Sister Emma, who knew my parents lived on a farm three miles out of town—not Africa—asked me why I would want to hurt peoples' feelings and make them appear foolish in front of their peers? Her clear disappointment in me was more painful than any punishment. And the disappointment didn't stop at school. The supper conversation centered on telling the truth and not hurting other people through our words and deeds. (What a long meal!) I learned a life-long lesson: If you don't tell the truth, it catches up with you.

This early lesson set the foundation for future business practices. Business is built on relationships, relationships are built on trust, and the foundation for trust is honesty. When you keep this principle in front of you, business is easy.

My first year in sales with Varsity Spirit Corporation, I opened forty new accounts. I was very excited with my success until it came time for delivery of our products. One of the factories was way behind in production and unfortunately most of my forty orders had landed there. I was tempted to fib and tell my new customers the factory had burned down or a hurricane had hit . . . anything other than the truth that we were having a lousy delivery year. But the vision of Sister Emma and that long dinner loomed in my head and I decided to be honest. Every Monday, I called my customers to let them know that their order was going to be delayed yet one more week. The customers didn't like the news; however, they did like that I was just telling them the plain, old truth. I lost only two accounts that year and I give the high retention rate in a tough situation to one selling skill: telling the truth.

Creating a Sales Culture of Truth Telling

When you sign on as a sales manager, you know that you will be using and applying new skills, such as hiring and selection, performance feedback, territory management, and setting goals. Most sales managers don't realize they will be charged with teaching their sales team an important sales skill: truth telling. Sales teams that seek and tell the truth are more productive, more relaxed, and have better business relationships.

So why is seeking the truth and dealing with the real issue so difficult for some salespeople? Here are some of my observations:

- **Salespeople are afraid of hearing the real answer, the truth.**
  They don't want to hear that the prospect is satisfied with his/her existing vendor because that means they will need to go out and find a new prospect. It is more comfortable spending time and energy creating proposals than creating new relationships.

- **Salespeople lack conviction about their sales process.**
  A good farmer follows a process each year to produce a good crop. In the spring, he plants and fer-

tilizes. He spends the summer months cultivating, irrigating, and spraying for weeds. And in the fall, he reaps a bountiful crop because he followed a system and didn't compromise or skip steps.

Good salespeople need to be just as dedicated to their sales process and not compromise or skip steps. When the prospect asks them for a proposal, before the salesperson has been allowed to ask questions, the salesperson needs to be upfront and truthful with prospects about their process and the need for conducting a "sales diagnostic" before providing a recommendation. The salesperson must be convinced enough about their process for developing business to pass on prospects who are not willing to engage in a consultative, partnership sales process.

Example: The prospect asks the salesperson to put together a proposal. Upon debriefing the call, you realize that the salesperson did not hear any evidence to support dissatisfaction with the prospect's current vendor. It's time to teach your rep to tell the truth and address the real issue.

Truth-telling response: "Mr. Prospect, I will be happy to put a recommendation together for you. However, I haven't heard any reasons why you need to leave your current supplier. They seem to be giving you excellent service, fair pricing, and are good at anticipating your needs. What am I missing?"

Rule: If you don't tell the truth, it always catches up with you. (Isn't your rep going to spend hours on a proposal for someone that has no reason to switch?)

Example: The prospect asks you to put together a recommendation but will not allow you to speak with the other decision makers.

Truth-telling response: "Mr. Prospect, I am going to decline turning in a recommendation. I can turn in a proposal; however, without input from the rest of the team, the proposal will be insufficient and miss hitting all company objectives."

Rule: If you don't tell the truth, it always catches up with you. (How many proposals with missing criteria has your team won?)

Get your sales team comfortable with seeking and telling the truth. It's amazing how this simple principle can increase sales.

The Truth-Telling Sales Manager

Telling the truth doesn't stop with sales and sales calls. Truth telling extends to sales management and leadership roles. I have had good mentors in my business career. These mentors are truth tellers, holding up a mirror to my weaknesses. One such mentor is Kline Boyd, my former boss. He was a gracious Southern gentleman. I was a young, brazen Midwesterner climbing the corporate ladder. More than once, Kline pulled me aside, pointing out how my direct style offended others. He continually reminded me to treat others the way I wanted to be treated. Did I always like hearing the truth? No. Did truth telling make me grow as a person and professional? Yes.

So why don't more leaders engage in truth telling? Truth telling is a great gift to the recipient; however, it can involve conflict. Many people equate conflict with hostility and anger. What most people don't understand is that relationships with any depth have probably experienced some kind of conflict. (Anyone reading this book *married?*) Conflict often is an opportunity for introspection, growth, and change.

Truth telling does not always win the popular vote. A sales manager's main role is to develop and grow people, both personally and professionally. That growth may come from teaching a salesperson how to work on a team to being more effective on a sales call to developing good work habits. It is not easy to tell someone the truth about their attitude, lack of sales skill, or poor time-management skills. But keep in mind, you may be the first sales manager that has told this salesperson the truth. You may be the first sales manager who cared enough about the salesperson to confront him or her with the reality of the situation. You may be the first sales manager that is helping this salesperson grow.

The foundation of business is relationships. Relationships are based on trust and trust comes from working with people and companies that tell the truth. Truth telling is an important principle to reinforce with your sales team. And it's an easy principle to execute because you don't have to remember anything but . . . the truth.

Lesson 6

The Empathetic Salesperson: Get "Other Focused"

It is easy to catch a "big fish, small pond" attitude growing up in a small town. This becomes even easier when you are good looking, charming, and athletic. My brother John had every reason in the world to feel like a "big fish," even a little arrogant. He was class president four years in a row, a gifted athlete, and blessed with movie star good looks. John never caught this syndrome; in fact, he was one of those rare individuals who paid attention to others and what they were feeling instead of being self-absorbed.

John was a gift to my family. He was killed in a car accident at the age of eighteen and like so many gifts, his gifts continued to give long after his death. We received many letters after John's death telling stories of John's ability to pay attention and make everyone feel important. My favorite story is from an individual I'll call Pete who was an underclassman when John was a senior.

Some of the high school bullies were picking on Pete and had great fun knocking schoolbooks out of his hands. Pete shared how John took the time to coach him on how to hold his books and hold his own. John couldn't catch the bullies every time, but he could help Pete play a little defense. John was empathetic. He seemed to understand what it felt like to be bullied, even though he had never personally experienced it.

Empathy and Professional Sales

Paying attention and empathy are two key qualities often missing from professional sales teams. Our teams get so well versed on product knowledge and slick presentation skills that they forget the most important part of building business and closing sales: caring about the prospect and his or her problems.

It looks something like this: The prospect shares a problem with the salesperson, such as decreased productivity caused by poor technology. The salesperson hears a "buying signal" and immediately starts buying that signal. The salesperson quickly starts presenting a fix to the problem, reciting the many features and benefits of his product or solution. The prospect gets a glazed look in his eyes because he really just wants someone to hear and feel his pain. He doesn't want a solution; he wants an empathetic ear and a salesperson who is genuinely interested in him and his problems.

Gerry Spence, a top trial lawyer in America, has not lost a civil jury trial since 1969. In his book, *Win Your Case,* he writes, "To move others we must first be moved. To persuade others, we must first be credible. To be credible we must tell the truth and the truth always begins with our feelings." Gerry Spence understands that if you can not step into another person's shoes, understand where he/she is coming from, why he/she is coming from that place, you will not be able to persuade or influence.

Top sales professionals understand the power of feeling others' pain, having empathy, and paying attention. These characteristics close more business than any overused sales technique.

How to Create a More Empathetic Sales Team

So how do you get your sales team to become empathetic and pay attention? There is good news and bad news. The bad news is you can't teach empathy; you must hire someone who has empathy because it is a sales skill that cannot be taught once someone has reached adulthood. Empathic people notice a flicker of the eye, a slight change in body language, and are highly in tune to how their words and actions affect others. The good news is that many salespeople have empathy but have buried this important talent after entering the sales profession. An insightful sales manager can uncover this lost skill by teaching his sales team patience and caring on a call. Yes, you read it right, *caring.* Caring about your prospect isn't taught in too many sales training programs; however, there is an old saying, "People don't care unless they know how much you care."

Make your team prove that they cared on a sales call. One of the easiest ways of proving that they cared is evaluating whether or not they listened on the call. Listening means getting rid of self-absorption and becoming "other focused." It means paying attention to something besides yourself and your products.

Ask your sales team if they took the time to listen and care enough to uncover the answers to the following questions:

- How long has this problem been an issue?
- How is it impacting the company? You?
- What is your biggest fear with this issue?
- What happens if the problem isn't fixed?
- What is making you take a look at it now?
- What has held you back from fixing the problem?

- What makes you think you lack the internal resources to fix it?

It is important to remind your sales team that asking questions, without proper intent, will come across as pure sales technique. I have seen many "technical" sales calls where salespeople do a great job of asking the right questions, the thought-provoking questions. However, it is evident that they really didn't care how the problem is affecting their prospect. They are listening to speak and it is apparent that they are there for one reason and one reason only: to get the sale. Without proper intent, prospects feel like they are taking part in a sales training role-play, not a partnership meeting to discuss issues and company goals.

Walk a mile in your prospect's moccasins. Show some empathy and pay attention to their problems, not just your solutions. You might be surprised at the business you close on the walk.

Lesson 7

Build Relationships: Put the Coffee On

Farming has changed a lot. Tractors have heated cabs, combines feature surround sound, and feeding livestock is automated (eliminating the necessity for hand feeding). Farming has become high tech. What hasn't become high tech on the farm are relationships. People still drive into a neighbor's yard and ask, "Got any coffee on?" There's no appointment set in Outlook or phone calls to confirm the meeting. Visiting with neighbors is just the way people in the heartland build relationships.

Norma Slotsve, a long-time friend, tells the story of her brother Buster Gullickson who farmed in Minnesota for more than fifty years. During those years, Buster changed his manual farming operation to a high-tech operation, feeding more than 1,000 head of cattle at a time. Eventually, he was shipping live cattle by air to Japan. What didn't change was the weekly meeting he held with his neighbors. Every Friday morning, they gathered in his Quonset to drink coffee, eat donuts, troubleshoot problems, and catch up.

Like everyone else, farmers have a million things vying for their attention; however, farmers seem to understand that if you are going to have friends and colleagues, you need to invest time in getting to know them. I think in the business world we call it building centers of influence and referral partnerships.

How to Build Business and Relationships

Technology has served us well in many ways. We can communicate across the world in seconds, access any information on the Internet, and develop products and services faster than before.

What technology has *not* been able to speed up is the development of solid business relationships. Unfortunately, too many salespeople think that because everything else is moving at the speed of light, so should the development of business relationships. The problem is, relationships are built on one key element: time. It takes time to know a person professionally and personally. Only when you know and trust a person will you do business or refer business to them.

Sales managers understand one of the key ways to build business is to develop referral partners and strategic alliances. Knowing this information is one thing; getting your sales team to do what it takes to develop meaningful relationships is another.

There are three important ingredients in building relationships:

1. **Get your sales team committed.**
   Good referral partners are as committed to growing their referral partners' businesses as they are to growing their own businesses. When attending association meetings or networking events, they are on the lookout for people or information that

will be of interest or value to their referral partners and/or customers.

Salespeople who excel at building relationships have a goal to be an extension of their referral partners' businesses because of the commitment to the relationship.

Your sales team may think they are practicing the principles of building relationships, however, actions speak louder than words. Ask your team if they can:

- Give their referral partners' thirty-second commercials? (If they can't describe the referral partners' businesses, how can they identify or provide an introduction?)

- Name the top three companies their referral partners have targeted for the year? (If a salesperson doesn't know the target, how can they look for opportunities and resources that help gain entry into the account?)

- State the referral partners' personal and professional goals? (If they don't know, how can they help them achieve?)

If your sales team doesn't know the answer to the aforementioned, or if any of the answers are "no," it is time to ask your team to evaluate their commitment to the referral relationship. Ask your team if they are investing enough time in "Friday morning coffee."

2. **Make sure your team is networking instead of not working.**

Leads groups are one of the many sales activities that salespeople attend with the goal of meeting referral partners. Don't get me wrong, leads groups are successful when they do what it takes to nurture relationships: time and work. One reason many leads groups produce less than positive results is that participants haven't committed to the time and work it takes to help their referral partners. Many groups confuse passing a pink slip of paper that says "use my name" with relationship building. This is not relationship building. This is an exercise in data transfer and the most work being done is punching up the contact information on a PDA. A salesperson who is truly interested in building relationships takes the time to make a call of introduction, deliver the referral partner's thirty-second commercial, and set up a personal introduction.

Study good friendships, good marriages, and good business relationships. The common theme in all three is investment of time and willingness to work at growing the relationship.

3. **Develop a plan to develop relationships.** Good sales professionals proactively plan their month. They know it takes a variety of prospecting activities to make a territory or business run—cold calls, networking, association meetings, and appointments. All are important activities focused on achieving results for the salesperson. But how many people on your team are setting aside time to pursue their most important prospecting activity—

the activity of helping referral partners grow their businesses?

Take a calendar review with each salesperson on your team. Review how much time he/she invested last month in activities related to building relationships with referral partners. Consider the following items:

- How many lunches did he/she set up to introduce referral partners to other partners, clients, or prospects?
- How many calls of introduction did he/she make on behalf of partners or clients?
- How many telephone calls/emails were sent informing referral partners and clients of an event that was of interest for them to attend?
- How often is he/she keeping referral partners posted on progress made on introductions they provided?

- How much time did he/she invest in sending thank you notes for the introductions? (Mom was right on this one, and the principle still holds.)

There is an old saying, "Tell me where you spend your time and money and I will tell you what your priorities are." In this age of information, you still need to invest in the number one thing that builds relationships—time. Can you smell the coffee?

Lesson 8

The Sun Doesn't Shine Everyday: Manage Results, Not Excuses

My mother and father taught me my earliest principles of leadership and management. They didn't impart these principles in formal meetings or with great rhetoric. I learned these lessons by observing their day-to-day actions in running a growing farm operation.

Every fall, my mother and father would spend long days in the field, harvesting the crops. That job was fraught with problems, usually caused by Mother Nature. Excessive rain, hail, or early snowfall caused delays but never deterred my parents from the outcome: getting the crops in. I never heard or saw them give into excuses such as, "Well, we just can't get the job done this year. The weather isn't cooperating.

We can't get the crops in." They could not—*would not*—accept excuses because the outcome was too important (feeding and clothing eight growing kids). They understood that businesses will encounter challenges on the way to hitting their goals. They also had a clear understanding that only the outcomes, not excuses, would be measured.

The Iowa harvest taught me a great business principle: Even though the "sun isn't shining," you must manage results, not excuses.

Managing Results, Not Excuses

Sales managers face a similar scenario because they must achieve a sales goal, despite business challenges. Often, a sales manager lays out sales goals only to find themselves dealing with excuses, however valid, from the sales team such as:

- I can't prospect because I am so busy putting out fires.
- No one is buying because of the economy, election, or war.

- Prospects are only buying on price.

Effective sales leadership is teaching your team that problems and excuses—rain and snow—will always be abundant for not "getting the crops in," for not reaching sales goals.

Great sales leaders are effective at getting their sales team to come up with the answer to the problem. This is based on the simple premise that people believe their own data, not yours. That means as a sales manager you must move out of "tell" mode and into "question" mode. Have your team answer the following questions to come up with their own data—their own plan—for moving past excuses:

1. I can't prospect because I am so busy putting out fires.

Coaching questions:

- Is your competitor going to quit prospecting because of similar fire-fighting issues?
- What systems can we create to prevent the fires?

- Realistically, are all fires going to go away? Is your sales goal going to go away? Is the company's need to grow revenue going to go away?

2. No one is buying because of the economy, election, war, etc.

Coaching questions:

- Is no one buying or are we just not finding the buyers who still have the budget and need?

- How must we change, as an organization, in order to close deals in a difficult buying situation?

3. Prospects are only buying on price.

Coaching questions:

- Are they buying on price or are we selling on price?

- If prospects are only buying on price, why are they continuing to have a dialogue with you, knowing the company is not the low-price provider?

- If the prospect is buying on price, are they really the ideal prospect for us to be pursuing? Shouldn't investment of time and resources be with prospects that value and are willing to pay for our services?

Effective sales leaders consistently remind their teams of the mindset and attitudes practiced by high-performance teams and individuals. Here are a few essentials:

1. **If it was easy, anyone could do it.**
   If going through "hell week" was easy, everyone would be a Navy Seal. If getting a Ph.D. was easy, there would be more than the current 1 percent of America's population possessing them. Elite sales teams are proud that they deal with problems better than the competition. Make sure your team realizes that hitting their sales goal is not the only indicator of success. It is also their attitude and ability to overcome problems on the way to achieving that goal that make up a true sales professional, an elite sales professional.

2. **Be an "all weather" player vs. a "fair weather" player.**

   The "fair weather" player does well when everything is going great at the company. Prospects are buying, customer service is following up, accounting is billing correctly, and the warehouse is shipping on time. However, the minute the weather turns bad, the "fair weather" player becomes part of the problem. He complains without offering solutions and expends his energy only in pointing fingers at other departments. The "all weather" player fares well in any kind of climate. Storm conditions don't affect her performance because she understands and lives the creed, "When the going get tough, the tough get going."

3. **Get real.**

   Show me a person or a company who is successful and I will show you a person or a company who has had as many setbacks as successes. It is unrealistic to think that everyday in business will be easy or good. Paul Stolz, author of *Adversity Quotient,* has studied top-performing companies and individuals from a variety of industries. The top trait found in all of these organizations and individuals is their ability to overcome adversity while other organizations gave into excuses.

Teach your sales team that the sun doesn't shine every day; that hail and rain occur in every position and every company. The elite sales team sows a crop and reaps a harvest, despite setbacks and obstacles.

Lesson 9

Field Sales Management: Start the Car

My father and mother worked everyday with us kids. The jobs varied from feeding cattle, cleaning out a feedlot, laundry, cleaning a room, or planting a garden. I never recall them pulling rank or refusing to do a job because they were the parents. On a farm, parents work side by side with their children. They don't sit in the farmhouse and give directions. They are outside everyday working in their business and spot problems early. My father could spot if a calf was getting ill or identify the first signs of crop failure. Farmers are smart business people because they spend time in their market everyday. They are truly "field managers."

Field Time vs. Office Time

Most salespeople begin their selling career in the field, spending time with customers and prospects. The successful salesperson often gets promoted to sales management and starts spending more time in the "white house," (the corporate office), compiling reports, attending internal meetings, and fire fighting. Less and less time is spent working side by side with sales teams meeting prospects and customers. White house syndrome sets in and pretty soon the sales manager has lost touch with reality. There is *nothing* that will replace face time with your sales team and with your customer. (Can you imagine a football coach trying to coach from his office?)

Avoiding the "Corporate White House"

Make it a priority to invest time each week with your sales team and customers. You will always have other priorities vying for your attention. Get used to it and get used to saying no to the attention grabbers of the "great indoors." Sales people don't work for companies; they work for people and will work harder for sales managers who care about them. And that caring doesn't show up in the form of a report; it comes in one format—time.

Real relationships develop during travel with your sales team. You will learn a side of them outside of work, have a chance to meet their families, and be present at serious reality checks provided by meetings with customers and prospects. Customers are the only reason we exist so doesn't it make sense that we invest time with the people who are keeping our business alive? High-level, corporate meetings are stimulating and fast-paced. The problem is that the meetings are with your peers, not your customers. Just like a good farmer, you need to get into the field and feedlot to keep a pulse on the latest trends and requests. A cow doesn't come to the farmer requesting medicine; don't expect your customers to come to you requesting new services.

The white house corporate seat will always be more comfortable. It is air conditioned, doesn't require the hassle of the airport or getting in and out of a car. The field car seat will always be your most profitable seat in the company because it provides you a front-row view necessary for leadership success—the view of your sales team and customers.

Show me a sales manager who has a good relationship with his team and I will show you a sales manager who's spending time in the field.

Lesson 10

Build Relationships, Part II: We've Got Company

Back home in Iowa, salespeople visited the farm, calling on both my mother and father. I often pose the question to my audiences at corporate trainings as to what name did my family give salespeople calling on a farming operation? Their responses include slick, greedy, or fast-talking. Not even close. We called salespeople *company.*

My parents felt that salespeople were partners in business who helped them with the day-to-day needs of a growing family and growing farm operation.

It has been thirty years since I have lived on a farm. However, I still remember two salesmen. Jerry McTigue was our Northwestern Mutual Life Insurance salesman. Jerry paid attention to the little details that make a big difference. Each year my seven siblings and I could count on a birthday card from Jerry. The card wasn't fancy, however, the attention made each of us feel special. Jerry was treated with respect and sold a lot of insurance. Today we call this type of selling partnership selling. Back then, it was just called good business.

The second salesperson frequenting our farm was our Fuller Brush salesman, Cletus Von Bank. He sold cleaning supplies and joined us for lunch on more than one occasion. I suspect he planned his travel schedule around lunch, knowing my mother was a great cook. Cletus was my mother's saving grace in trying to keep an old farmhouse, occupied by ten people, clean. He always brought the latest cleaning miracles to my mother. (Not to mention much needed adult conversation!)

I don't recall hearing my parents discuss how they were going to get Jerry or Cletus to discount their prices. They believed if you wanted good service, you paid for good service. They believed in treating others the way they wanted to be treated—with fairness and respect.

Business Partnerships and Company Profitability

I have observed a clear link between how a company treats its vendors and profitability. Companies that treat vendors with disrespect generally lose in the long run. Service begins to slip, collaboration goes away, and the hidden costs in turning over vendors slowly erodes at its margins.

Here is an example of a local company that "gets" business partnerships. Land Title Guarantee is a successful title company in Denver, Colorado, with whom I have had the privilege of working with for many years.

Brian Hamiliton, one of Land Title's principals, shared the company philosophy with me. "If your mission statement says you value people, you must value all people, including members of your internal team, vendors, and alliance partners." Brian went on to tell me that people and partnerships have been the core value at Land Title for more than thirty-seven years. Bill Vollbracht, founder of the company, insists that vendors be paid not just on time, but early. At Land Title, invoices are paid within ten days of receipt. In their words, "we know our vendors—our partners—have a business to run and bills to pay, just like we do."

Vendors enjoy working with Land Title and feel like their work is valued. And when a vendor feels valued, they are loyal and work to deliver the very best in products, service, and quality.

Western Paper Distributors, a rapidly growing distribution company also in Denver, is another example of a company that understands partnering with their vendors. Their manufacturer representatives and management team are invited each year to the Western Paper national sales meeting. Western Paper openly speaks to their sales team and vendors about successes and failures of the previous year. Nick Morris, president of Western Paper, says, "Our suppliers are an extension of our sales arm. Business is a two-way street in which both parties need to be committed to helping each other grow. Nickel and diming a vendor isn't going to create that type of partnership."

Heartland Principles for Building Partners

The number one rule in developing partners is to practice the golden rule of sales: treat your vendors as you would like to be treated. Vendors are like every other human being on earth; they thrive on appreciation and recognition. (I should know . . . I am one.)

Here are ideas that I have gleaned from organizations that practice the golden rule and build successful partnerships:

- **Create a vendor appreciation program.** Give a "vendor of the year" award to the company that has gone above and beyond the call of duty to help your company achieve its goals.

- **Invite your top vendors to your holiday party.**
  You're sending a message to your vendor that he/she is valued and an integral part of your company's team.

- **Write a thank you note to your top partners.**
  Business is a two-way street. As a good salesperson, we are taught to thank our customers. Become a good customer and thank your vendors for going the extra mile.

- **Include vendors in your annual planning meetings.**
  Let them know the corporate objectives and how they play into achieving those objectives.

Showing appreciation and making others feel valued yields a great return on investment for your company. Make your vendors part of your sales team. Their extra effort and commitment to the organization will show up "in the black" on your company balance sheet.

Lesson 11

Do Your Chores

I knew that farm chores were a part of everyday life. Chores changed, depending on your age, but the expectation of completing them did not. Cleaning the house on Saturday morning was a ritual in our home. No play was allowed until the cleaning was done. Tantrums, faked illness, or comparisons to kids that didn't have chores did nothing to deter my mother from having us complete our mission.

I distinctly remember trying to frustrate mom into dismissing my chores. I was charged with vacuuming three sets of stairs and got the big idea if I banged the vacuum loudly on each stair, she would come running and tell me to stop. Mom was either deaf or patient because she allowed the banging to go on until I wore myself out. I accepted the obvious. I didn't have to like chores; I just had to do them.

There was also a clear expectation established around the *quality* of completing those chores. Mom would explain, in detail, how she wanted the job completed. She didn't take for granted that we knew how to complete the chore to satisfaction. She took the time to show us how to fold clothes, dust, and vacuum. Shortcuts and sloppiness? Mother dealt with that quickly by reassigning the same chore until it was up to standard. In business today, we use terms such as "accountability" and "benchmarking" to describe my mother's management style.

Sales Management and "No Option" Behavior

Just like a good parent, sales managers must impress two important principles to their team. The first is "no option" behavior. Just like housecleaning, there are chores in every professional's life he/she doesn't enjoy. Accountants dislike the hours of tax seasons; doctors dislike the headache of insurance paperwork.

Salespeople dislike cold calling. Professional service firms don't enjoy networking.

Remind your team they don't have to like it; they just have to do it. Great sales people make one last stop after a long day of meetings. Top producers rehearse a sales presentation one more time. Top salespeople attend networking events, even when they are tired and don't feel like talking to one more person. High-performance sales teams understand that everything in sales is not going to be fun—you do it anyway.

Expect the Best and Get the Best

The second principle top sales managers teach and enforce is setting crystal clear expectations. Mom didn't take it for granted that we knew how to complete a task to satisfaction; sales managers shouldn't take it for granted that their salespeople possess the knowledge and skills needed to succeed on your team.

Measurements for success must be defined in four core areas: company values, a sales activity plan, sales skills, and sales results.

1. **Company values.**

   Company values often lack measurement. An organization may say they value commitment, but never clearly define what commitment looks like. I was working with Sue Holland, president of ETI, in putting measurements to their company values. During the workshop, the word "commitment" was being tossed around rather loosely as one of the core values. I challenged the team to be more specific and finally a light bulb went on. A team member spoke up and said, "Commitment at ETI means when there is a snow storm in Denver, I set my alarm for four o'clock in the morning instead of six o'clock to make sure I am at my desk to serve our customers." Commitment could now be expected, measured, and duplicated at this company. By the way, this same company was named Small Business of the Year by the South Metro Denver Chamber in 2005. Do you think having clear values is part of the reason for their success?

2. **A well-defined sales activity plan.**
   Sales activity plans need specific measurement and individualization for each member on your team. The customization depends on their experience, type of territory, and customer base. Get specific about below average, good, and excellent performance. The more specific your expectations are, the more self-directed your sales team will become. The following is an example of a clearly defined sales activity plan for a new salesperson:

Cold Calling:

25 cold calls each day = "A" level sales activity

15 cold calls each day = "B" level sales activity

10 cold calls each day = "C" level sales activity

Association Meetings:

Running a committee = "A" level involvement

Serving on a committee = "B" level involvement

Showing up at a meeting = "C" level involvement

The salesperson is very clear on the sales activity needed for success. They understand that "A" level activity yields "A" level results, which also yields "A" level commissions!

3. **Sales skills.**
   You can use the same formula in making sure your team is getting smarter and applying proven sales skills. Companies waste thousands of dollars on sales training if they never set an expectation for learning and applying material.

If you want to study application of knowledge and skills, study a good football team. You can't just be a "big, dumb guy" and play ball anymore. There are too many plays that need to be memorized and executed. Can you imagine the quarterback yelling out a play and the rest of the football team saying, "Huh? I don't remember how to do that play"? It may sound a little far fetched but think about an identical scenario in sales when the prospect asks the salesperson to tell him or her about the company and the salesperson can't deliver the appropriate commercial for the industry or level of decision making. They don't know the "thirty-second commercial" play.

Crystal clear expectations for learning a "thirty-second commercial" look like this:

Week One:
Turn in your written thirty-second commercial.
= "C" level skill

Week Two:
Be prepared to deliver your thirty-second commercial from memory. (Remember the football analogy.)
= "B" level skill

Week Three:
Be prepared to deliver your thirty-second commercial and transition into probing questions.
= "A" level skill

With these formulas, the salesperson is very clear on the skills needed to be an "A" player on your team. And conversely, the skills that label you as a "C" player.

- **Product knowledge.**
  Product knowledge is essential in order for the salesperson to connect the "pain or problem" of the prospect with intelligent recommendations. The problem is lack of expectation and inspection of that product knowledge. Set expectations for learning product knowledge in three areas:

- **What they need to know and when they need to know it.**
  There is so much information to learn that sales representatives have a hard time prioritizing learning objectives and focus on the wrong information. Help your team get clear on the most important knowledge needed to succeed with their clients.

Salespeople are only human and they will procrastinate without a deadline. As sales manager, you must lay out a plan for learning. Define what the salesperson is expected to know at the end of four weeks, three months, and six months. Remember, you get what you expect.

- **Retrieval of sales and product knowledge.** Give tests to your team to make sure they can retrieve knowledge gained during training seminars. If a salesperson can't retrieve it on a written test or role play, they certainly can't retrieve it during a sales call.

- **Application of product knowledge.** Once the knowledge is memorized, create case studies to see if the salesperson knows how to choose the right product and selling solution that aligns with the problem experienced by the prospect.

4. **Sales Results.** Most companies focus on the sales quota, period. Then they can't figure out why they are not growing a particular market, product, or margins. Get crystal clear on what type of sales results you are looking for. If you are at the early stages of growth, you may just want sales in the door and don't care what is being sold or who it's being sold to. As the company grows, it becomes important to expand certain markets niches, products, and margins.

I remember trying to grow outerwear sales at Varsity. We gave extra samples to the sales reps, provided training, and even featured the outerwear on two extra pages in the catalog. It was only when I attached a specific goal, by region and rep, that significant growth was achieved.

To get specific growth, you must get specific. Set a sales goal for each of the previous three items within the overall sales goal. Salespeople pay attention to what is expected and measured. If you don't get specific, here's what you can expect—not much.

It's time to get the sales chores done. If you want to "play in the big leagues," teach and enforce "no option" behavior. Get clear on what you expect, measure what you expect, and watch your team exceed what you expect!

Lesson 12

Team Motivation: Get a Mission

Okoboji and Arnold's Park are two names synonymous with fun in northwest Iowa. Okoboji is a popular summer resort and Arnold's Park is an amusement park.

Arnold's Park is Iowa's local Disney World. It has rides, roller coasters, and bumper cars, to boot. Each summer, Arnold's Park partnered with the Pepsi Corporation in a promotion called Pepsi Days. If you collected a certain amount of Pepsi caps, you were rewarded with a certain number of free ride tickets at Arnold's Park. (For the young readers, there was a day when everyone drank Pepsi out of a bottle, not a can.) Each summer, my siblings joined forces and collected as many Pepsi caps as possible. We pooled our resources and banded together for a common goal: a fun day at Arnold's Park. Who would have guessed that collecting Pepsi caps would teach me one of the greatest tools for motivating sales teams: rallying the team around a mission, a common goal.

The number one question I am asked by sales managers is: "How do I motivate my team?"

Let's clear up a misconception—you can't motivate a salesperson. You must hire someone with motivation. (My parents were not holding sales meetings inspiring us to collect Pepsi caps. They didn't have to. We were highly self-motivated and took it upon ourselves to bug everyone we could about giving their Pepsi caps to us.)

With that said, it is an inherent part of your job to create an environment that sustains and encourages motivation, one that keeps the motivated individual even more motivated.

There are several types of motivation. One type is fear and it can work—i. e., you're going to lose your job, be demoted, or lose commissions. Fear, however, is short lived and does not improve or sustain motivation. Another type is incentive. Incentives, both tangible and non-tangible, work fairly well. Trips, awards, and public recognition are very successful in creating and sustaining motivation. The third type of motivation is even more powerful than incentives. It is rallying your team behind a mission, a common goal. When sales teams rally around a common goal, look out, because the unachievable gets achieved. Energy is created by unifying everyone's efforts behind a common goal. Energy creates emotion, which creates action: a powerful partnership. The trip to Arnold's park was a great incentive, however, the real momentum came from all of us counting our Pepsi caps each day, working toward our mission: a FREE day of fun at the park.

Take a look at the NFL. It's a great example of teams working toward a common goal, a mission. What else could make grown men go out and get beat up every Sunday afternoon? Sure, they get paid the big bucks, but what really keeps them going? Every member on the team is driving toward a common goal, the goal of winning the Super Bowl.

I became familiar with the power of "mission" as a regional sales manager for Varsity. Year after year, the Southwest region came in as the number one region in the company. And by all rights, they should have. Cheerleading and sports are huge in the South. The squads ordered often and ordered a lot. On the other hand, the Midwest region was comprised of smaller schools that didn't order every year and the average order size was smaller. How could the Midwest region possibly beat the Southwest region? I made beating the Southwest our mission, our common goal. My sales team and I decided there was just one thing in our selling life that year—beating the Southwest region. Every conference call and meeting ended with all of us holding up our index finger saying, "There's just one thing we are going to do this year. *Beat the Southwest region.*" We squeaked by the Southwest region that year beating them by a mere $10,000 dollars. (Mission impossible just made possible by having a mission!)

Creating a "Mission" at Your Sales Organization

So how do you create a mission? A common goal? It's really unlimited because you get to decide. Do you want to be number one? Or do you want to be the Microsoft of your industry? Are there certain values you want your organization to be known for?

The following are components for creating a mission:

- **Define the mission/goal.**
  We want to be the number one branch in the country. We want to be the most skilled sales professionals on the street. We want to be the "go-to" sales team. The common goal is determined by what's important to you and your team.

- **Beat the goal drum until you can't hear it anymore.**
  You can't talk about the goal, the mission, and then walk away from it. Become obsessed by it and remind your team of the goal in every conversation, memo, or email. What you and your team think,

you will become. Jack Welch, former CEO of GE, made it his mission to create boundaryless environments at GE. His goal was to create a business environment where best practices were shared from other divisions and companies. He beat the "goal drum" by having teams at GE wake up everyday to the motto, "Finding a Better Way Every Day."

- **Develop rituals around the mission.**
  Let's go back to football. Think of all the great rituals surrounding football. First, there is a team name and a mascot. People love buying "stuff" that supports the team and mascot. Use the same concept and create "stuff" to support your goal. If you want to be number one in the country, buy everyone a jersey with "#1" on it. Or send an email every Monday morning with nothing on it but a big "#1."

Another ritual connected with football is tailgating. Football fans assemble and get ready to support the mission: winning the game, which leads to winning the Super Bowl. Create your own version of tailgate parties by transforming your sales meetings into goal meetings.

Talk about what it means to be number one, what it takes to earn the number one spot. Show movies like *Glory Days* or *Hoosiers*, which show athletes who came from behind to be number one in their class.

- **Track it and share it.**
  Think of the fervor surrounding favorite football teams. All die-hard football fans know the stats of their favorite team. Let your team know how close they are to achieving their mission, their common goal.

- **Celebrate it.**
  When you achieve the goal, hold a "Super Bowl" party. Include trophies, speeches, and champagne. You may even want to get your own version of a Super Bowl ring!

Become a master motivator by rallying your sales team behind a mission, a common goal. Mission impossible will become possible.

Lesson 13

Build A Winning Team, Heartland Style

I am sure my parents didn't even know the concept of team building; however, they managed to practice key principles of building synergistic teams in managing a large family. A big family requires teamwork. There is too much work for one person; therefore, everyone pitches in to make sure to get a job done.

For example, meal preparation for ten people every night was quite a project. (This on top of eight loads of laundry and eight sets of homework.) My mother used her project management, delegation, and conflict-management skills in pulling off this feat flawlessly each night. One child was in charge of vegetable preparation, another in charge of setting the table, another in charge of serving, and another in charge of clean up. The goal was dinner and each child was assigned a specific job to accomplish the goal. We knew that if one of us fell short on our assignment, we wouldn't be sitting down together at the dinner table. Being kids, we always thought someone else's chore was easier or more fun. My mother quickly solved this problem by rotating chores. We quickly learned that the "grass is not greener on the other side of the fence" and asked for a transfer back to the original job!

Little did I know that dinner preparation was teaching me great skills for interfacing with other departments in achieving future corporate goals.

Creating High-Performance Sales Teams and Teamwork

Two important elements are critical in building teamwork:

- Realization that each department in the company needs the other department in order to beat the competition.

- Every person's job is important and has its challenges and perks.

Varsity Spirit Corporation succeeded because early members of the executive team valued the importance of each person's job and the importance of working together. We didn't operate in "business silos" worrying only about our department's goals. We knew that every department needed to deliver in order to put "food on the table."

As vice president of sales, I was responsible for making sure my sales team hit their sales goal. I was also responsible for making sure my reps turned in clean, accurate orders so order entry could achieve their daily goal of orders processed. Sales also needed to be forecast accurately so other departments could staff up and inventory could be ordered and managed.

The order entry department was responsible for entering the data in an accurate and timely fashion. They also provided daily reports to the sales team so they could quote accurate delivery dates to their customers.

The production department worked around the clock to hit delivery dates and also provided daily updates on delivery to insure that the reps could give accurate information and top customer service to our customers.

All members of the Varsity team executed different chores in order to get "food on the table." No job was considered more important than another because all departments needed to succeed in order to satisfy and retain the customer.

Teaching Respect for Others' Chores

High-performance teams make sure all members of the team appreciate and respect the "chores" of other team members. It's an excellent idea to require that new hires work in each department of the company. Two things happen: the new hire has a better understanding of the entire business, and also sees how his or her actions impact another member of the team.

This temporary internship "is a must" for building synergistic teams, particularly between sales and customer service. It is easy for customer service to envy the sales team, thinking they are conducting social calls all day long. That is until the customer service rep spends a day getting in and out of a hot car, spending down time in an airport, or dealing face to face with a demanding customer.

On the other hand, sales teams perceive customer service as an easy job—just picking up the phone and taking service calls or orders. After a couple of days in customer service, they quickly understand the stress of working in an environment where the phone doesn't quit ringing and the customer doesn't quit demanding. It also gives the salesperson a first-hand understanding of why customer service can't rush every order.

Amazing how attitudes change when you make your teams "walk a mile in each others' shoes." Each person quickly learns that the grass isn't greener on the other side of the fence. If you want good teams, if you want to win, make sure that everyone respects and appreciates their fellow teammate's chores.

Lesson 14

I Hear Your Actions: Walk the Talk

Many people have heard of detassling corn in Iowa; however, most people have not heard of bean walking. Bean walking (now extinct) is the sweat-inducing job of walking up and down bean rows, hoeing out weeds to produce a greater yield at harvest. One evening, after a full day of bean walking, my father loaded all my siblings in the car and drove to the bean field to inspect our work. One of my brothers was rather sloppy in his work that day, leaving tall weeds in his assigned rows. My father asked my brother (no name to protect the innocent) to re-walk his rows. We sat in the car watching my brother re-walk his missed rows for about an hour. My father didn't deliver a huge lecture on right and wrong or rant and rave about the sloppy work. His actions—simply sitting in the car—spoke louder than any words, telling us if the job wasn't done right, it would be done again and again, until it was right.

Aligning Your Words and Actions as a Sales Leader

Companies have profit and loss (P & L) statements that show how the company is performing against plan. It's too bad there isn't a line on the P & L statement that captures the amount of dollars lost due to poor alignment between words and actions. A colleague of mine aptly describes this as "mission statements on the wall that never hit the office halls."

There are two areas where sales organizations can misalign. The initiation process of new sales recruits is a classic example. The mission statement at the company might read that, "people are the company's biggest asset." Yet there is no investment in sales training, technology training, or product knowledge training. The new salesperson is enrolled in the "sink or swim" training program and given a life preserver as their first briefcase.

Accountability for actions is the second area of misalignment in sales organizations. Each department in the company is required to turn in reports showing progress against goals. When the same accountability is requested of salespeople in the form of call reports or forecasting, they push back, complaining of micromanagement or no time. The weak sales manager caves in and the mission statement at the company is revised to read, "We are accountable to actions, except if you are in the sales department. Then, just do whatever you want and the rest of us will keep our fingers crossed hoping that you are staying focused on the right things." (Can you imagine the shipping department saying they don't want to turn in reports for the number of units shipped against plan and stating, "We feel like you don't trust us when you ask for a report.")

Choose your words carefully and stand by those words. There is no quicker way to lose credibility as a leader to say one thing and deliver another. Organizations that are well aligned consistently do two things:

1. **Make no exceptions to honoring the mission and values of the organization.** While coaching at University of Arkansas, Lou Holtz benched three of his top players before the Orange Bowl. The reason: they were consistently late for practice, actions that disrupted the rest of the team and were not in alignment with the values and missions of the organization. (Keep in mind that these three players represented 78 percent of the touchdowns made so far that year.) Lou Holtz understands leadership and the importance of aligning words and actions, especially in tough predicaments. By benching his top players, Lou Holtz honored his conviction of not making short-term decisions that jeopardize long-term gains. Lou Holtz wasn't just trying to win one game, he was building a team, building a culture. The rest is history: Lou Holtz led the University of Arkansas to win the 1977 Orange Bowl.

Sales managers are tempted by a similar situation that I call the "golden handcuff" scenario. You have a top producer who is generating great revenue *and* great headaches at the company. The headaches vary from abusing the customer service department to writing up sloppy orders to not completing necessary forecasting reports. This scenario is where many sales managers fall short on alignment. They keep the top producer even though he or she does not honor the company's mission statement of respecting and valuing others. This sales manager will achieve some short-term goals but will never build a high-performing sales culture because the rest of the sales team knows their manager is bound to "golden handcuffs." Sales teams don't respect leaders wearing that kind of jewelry!

2. **Reinforce the mission statement and the organization's values. Often.**

Dan Carrison and Rod Walsh are the authors of *Semper Fi*, a business book based on principles learned while both men were in the Marine Corps. The Marine Corps are highly trained fighting units and are usually the first sent into battle. The Marines want you thinking like a Marine and cannot afford someone in battle who does not know how to respond under fire. They drill their mission, values, and tactics into recruits twenty-four hours a day. As part of boot camp, a drill sergeant will stop a private and ask him to recite, on the spot, one of a hundred phrases that are expected to be memorized from the *Guide Book for Marines.*

Sales organizations can learn from the Marines. How many sales managers can walk up to a member of the sales team and ask him/her to state the core values of the company or the company's value proposition? Try this "sales Marine" pop quiz at your company:

- Private, give me your thirty-second commercial.
- Private, throw out the number one objection heard in our business and the appropriate response.
- Private, what are the core values of this company?
- Private, who are your top ten targets for the year?

- Private, who are your top ten clients and how are you servicing them?

A well-known saying is, "Your actions speak so loudly I can't hear what you are saying." As a leader, you must make sure you draw a straight line between your words and actions. Top sales producers don't respect or follow crooked lines.

Lesson 15

Get Nosy: Know Your Customers' Business

I often hear the complaint about small towns that everyone knows your business . . . even before you do! People in small towns are curious about other people's lives, families, and business. In fact, they can get down right nosy in a small town. However, the longer I have been in sales consulting and training, the more convinced I am that some of my best sales training came from the early years of listening to "nosy" conversations. I learned to be curious, question, and be interested in people and . . . their business.

Here is what a typical "nosy" conversation sounds like in a small town. Read carefully and notice how the conversation includes all the basics of a good consultative sales call.

"Well, I understand the Browns are getting a new car." **(Prospect need is uncovered.)**

"I wonder why they think they need a new car. Just what do they think a new car will do for them?" **(Probing questions.)**

"Well, maybe they need a car that is faster. Hmm, maybe the other one is uncomfortable to sit in."

"Oh, I bet they just want to upgrade their image."

"No, I think that old car is a gas guzzler." **(Decision criteria.)**

"Well, how does Betty feel about that process?"

"Oh, she feels fine about it. In fact, Betty told me they are going to spend more money than they ever had on a car. Can you see Fred's face about now?" **(Decision and budget step.)**

Ok, ok, the conversation is a stretch. But think about it. The people in the conversation are not trying to come up with a solution, they are too busy asking questions—being nosy—to go into product dump mode.

Creating a "Nosy" Sales Culture

Salespeople seem to lose their curiosity as they evolve into adulthood. Instead of nosing around when a prospect shares a problem, they tend to go into presentation mode, too often and too soon resulting in no sale. Forget high-tech training and bring in some fun if you want to create a "nosy" sales culture.

Stage your next sales meeting at a local coffee shop in a small town. Ask each rep to come to the meeting prepared to share the results of a first meeting with a prospect. Go to the local party store and buy some big noses. After each salesperson has shared their story, have the rest of the team put on their nose prop. It is a great visual and people learn best when they are having fun. Have the team get nosy by asking questions in small town language:

- "Now, why do you suppose they are addressing the problem now?"
- "Now, just what do you think will happen if they don't fix the problem?"
- "Well, good grief, why haven't they fixed the problem?"
- "Sure, but are they willing to commit the time and money to fix? You know how cheap they can be!"
- "Don't you think they are getting worried for nothing? I mean what's the worse thing that can happen if they don't fix the problem?"

Continue the fun theme and hold a contest. Divide your sales team into two teams. Present a prospect's problem to each group and have a contest to see which team can ask the most questions around the problem without presenting a solution. The team that asks the most questions is the winner.

Create a monthly "journalist" award and present it to the salesperson who consistently provides answers to the who, what, when, where, why, and how of the prospect's problem:

- Who else is being affected?
- What else is being affected?
- When are they looking to solve the problem?
- Where else in the organization is the problem making an impact?
- Why are they looking to solve now?
- How much is the problem costing them?

Get a small town attitude on your sales team. Make it your sales team's business to know their customer's business!

Lesson 16

Get Off the Phone

Every generation will have its tale of hardship: no television to watch, no transportation to school other than walking three miles, and, my favorite, no telephone line other than the party line.

Back on the farm, the telephone party line meant that five farm families shared one phone line. Any member of the five families could listen to each others' conversations. As kids, we took great delight in listening to our teenage siblings as they swooned and crooned with boyfriends or girlfriends. Our fun never lasted for long as we were busted fairly soon because of our giggles and commentary. "Get off the phone" ended our eavesdropping fairly quickly. Following the bust, parents gave us lessons in telephone etiquette.

As much as some things change, some things remain the same. Today, sales managers are charged with the same job as our parents were years ago: teaching phone etiquette to their teams.

Cell Phones: Etiquette and Lost Sales

Corporate America is losing thousands of sales dollars to L. O. A. D.: lack of attention disorder. Salespeople pride themselves on their ability to multitask; however, they don't realize they are multitasking themselves right out of relationships and sales.

Salespeople are starting to remind me of dogs on shock collars. The minute the phone rings or vibrates, they feel compelled to answer or check the phone—regardless of what they are doing or who they are with. Let's say a salesperson is calling on a prospect. The salesperson is doing a very good job of building rapport. The prospect is feeling comfortable, thinking this salesperson really does care about his/her problem. Then the salesperson's cell phone vibrates. The salesperson looks down to check who is calling and rapport is broken because the prospect receives the real message: You are important, but not more important than an incoming call.

A colleague shares a story of a breakfast meeting with a potential referral partner. They were ten minutes into breakfast when the possible referral partner took a phone call. This was not an emergency call, just a phone call. As my colleague sipped her coffee, alone, she made a mental note to put this possible referral candidate in the "just doesn't get building relationships" file. My colleague had scheduled an hour out of her busy day to meet this person and expected full attention during that hour. The phone-addicted salesperson couldn't resist the distraction and as a result, lost out on an opportunity to build a relationship.

Bill Clinton (put aside personal and political opinions) is a master at paying attention and not allowing outside distractions to interfere in his communication with people. He has a reputation for building incredible rapport with people in a short amount of time. People that have met Bill Clinton share similar comments such as, "I felt like I was the only person in the room. He made me feel so important. He is intent on every word that you say." (Get the feeling he isn't checking his cell phone or PDA?)

Turn off your cell phone. Yes, you read the statement correctly. Any veteran of sales knows the old adage, "People buy from people they like." And guess what? People like people who pay attention to them.

Cell Phones: Focus and Increased Revenues

Successful salespeople have the ability to stay focused on activities needed to achieve goals. This proven concept for success is being threatened by the cell phone. Because of the 24/7 access by colleagues, customers, and prospects, a salesperson can spend his/her entire day responding to calls rather than building new relationships. Time management and working a plan goes right out the window because the only plan in place is answering phone calls. Don't get me wrong, returning phone calls, in a timely manner, is essential in running a good business; so is organizing your day and building in set times to make and return phone calls.

It was this very reason that I was brought into work with a sales group selling promotional products. The sales team spent their entire day in reactive, trouble-shooting mode. Because they were always answering their cell phones, they could not get focused enough to make outbound, prospecting calls. Sales were stagnant because the team was caught in the modern day "sales rat on treadmill with a cell phone."

The owner and I reached a compromise with the sales team that met the need for client care and the owners' need for new business. The sales team promised to take two hours every day and focus on prospecting for new business. They did not take any incoming calls during those two hours. To make sure they were not alienating customers, the team was allowed to check voicemail at the end of each hour. Any true emergencies were handled or delegated at that time. The sales team discovered that the customers still felt taken care of, even if the call was returned sixty minutes later. They also discovered that sixty minutes of uninterrupted, focused phone prospecting yielded new clients and larger paychecks.

We have come a long way from the party line—or have we? Maybe it's time to get your sales team "off the phone." Hold a phone etiquette class during your next sales meeting and teach your team manners and focus. It's a very easy way to increase sales.

Lesson 17

Achieve Your Sales Quota and Fun Quota

As much as I remember working as a kid, I also remember playing a lot. We built tree forts in the summer and snow castles in the winter. Neighborhood kids gathered for a game of kick the can or re-enact the latest episode of *Daniel Boone.* Fun started early in the morning and finished late at night. I guess we knew about "balance" before it became a *buzzword.* We practiced it by making sure we achieved our fun quota as well as our work quota.

Achieving the Sales Quota and Fun Quota

Sales managers invest a lot of time in showing their sales team how to build relationships and close business to achieve the ultimate: the sales quota. Sales managers often forget that an important component of hitting the sales quota is accomplished by achieving the fun quota. When is the last time your sales team hit their fun quota?

- **Fun will . . . put problems in perspective.** During my years as vice president of sales and marketing for Varsity Spirit Corporation, we had several years where we grew 25 to 30 percent. We did our best to build an infrastructure to handle the growth; however, we had years where we fell short in hitting production and delivery deadlines. One year, in particular, we fell short in delivering stock items because of a small warehouse and lack of a sophisticated pick and pack system. The sales team was coming into the national sales meeting tired and frustrated. We hit our sales quota that year; now, we needed to hit the fun quota.

  Prior to the national sales meeting, Varsity solved the order-fulfillment problem by expanding into a larger warehouse and investing in state-of-the-art shipping technology. The national sales meeting could have opened with a serious message from the president on warehouse improvements and commitment to excellence. Instead, we decided to start the meeting with fun—poking fun at ourselves while introducing improvements.

The meeting opened with a lively video of me stuffed into a small shipping container, giving the sales team a tour of the new-and-improved warehouse. I looked ridiculous stuffed in the small container; however, we achieved the goal of fun. The sales team laughed and cheered while learning of improvements we made at the corporate office to insure ease of sales the following year.

- **Fun will . . . stop the insanity. (Insanity is repeating the same behavior . . . and you know the rest.)**

A client of mine, Corporate Express, acquired one of its competitors and with that acquisition came the customers of the competitor. Or so they thought. Unfortunately, no one prepared the acquired clients and they refused to speak with their newly appointed sales representative. Repeated phone calls and letters of introduction were falling on deaf ears with the new customers. The "tried and true" methods of transitioning customers weren't working so it was time to stop the insanity and try some fun.

In a brainstorming session with the sales team, we developed off-the-wall, fun strategies for diffusing the hostile acquired customers. One sales representative showed up to an appointment with a "bull's eye" pinned to the front of her jacket. Another sales representative arrived with ice cream cones, informing the receptionist she needed to see her new customer right away—before the ice cream melted. The hostile customers couldn't help but laugh, enjoy themselves, and invite the fun-loving sales representatives in for a short visit. New relationships started because fun was the goal, not sales.

You can take the same approach with a sales task that is not necessarily fun. Cold calling can either be drudgery or fun. When I started in the sales training business, I made twenty-five cold calls a day. One of the most successful scripts sounded like this: "Hi, it's Colleen Stanley. You don't know me and I will be real up front with you … this is a cold call."

Believe it or not, 95 percent of the time the response was a laugh and permission to speak. I was having fun and so was the prospect.

Make Failure Fun

How many of you are tired of hearing, "You learn more from your failures than your successes . . . don't take failure personally?" If this is true, why aren't companies and sales teams just leaping at failing?

Take time during sales meetings to review "war stories." Encourage your team to laugh about mishaps that occurred during a sales call. When the team learns to lighten up, they also learn that a mistake is not life or death. Mistakes are a part of growing a business and growing professionally.

A colleague of mine, Rick Davis, models failure and fun by sharing the story of his first sales call with his training audience. Rick showed up to his first sales appointment with a shiny, new briefcase. He asked good questions and built rapport with the prospect, resulting in a sale. The problem was that Rick didn't know the combination to his brand new briefcase and couldn't access the documents to write up the order! Embarrassing, yes. Funny, yes. Lessons learned, yes. Rick's point to his students is that it is ok not be perfect. You'll still close business.

Here are some tips to building a sales organization that hits both the sales *and* fun quota:

- **Incorporate fun into your sales meetings.** Rent a movie such as *Tommy Boy,* which illustrates poor, outdated selling methods. You can use the clip to point out the good, the bad, and the ugly of selling techniques.

- **Recognize and appreciate failure.**
  Give rewards to salespeople who bring the best war story to your meeting. Start a special office display representing risk taking, lessons learned, and not taking failure too serious.

- **Make learning fun.**
  Play Family Feud or Jeopardy when teaching your team new product knowledge or sales knowledge.

- **Have an all-team phone blitz day.**
  All members of the team are in the office making cold calls. During the blitz, have senior executives on hand to fetch coffee and donuts. Role reversal is always fun!

Practice balance with your sales team. If you want to hit your sales quota, make sure that your team is hitting their fun quota!

Lesson 18

I Dare You: Do Something That Scares You

Risk taking is one of the more important principles I learned growing up in Iowa, and I have to give credit to my brothers for their one-on-one coaching in this area.

There are many books written on birth order and the corresponding characteristics that accompany that placement. I am grateful that my birth order dropped me smack in the middle of four brothers.

At an early age, I learned to be gender blind. My brothers didn't care if I was a girl; they only cared if I could keep up with their antics and activities. More than once, I remember participating in a game of "Dare" with my brothers. The dare varied from hanging by my knees from a tree branch to crawling across the roof of a building. (And no, our parents were not privy to the game.) The "Dare" game taught me to try things that appeared scary, and as a result grew my confidence because I succeeded at the scary thing and got out of my comfort zone. (Ever been 100 feet up in the air climbing up a barn rope?) The "Dare" game also has its place in high-performance sales teams.

Building a "Dare Devil" Sales Team

Any good coach knows his greatest challenge lies in having individuals achieve what they don't think they are capable of achieving. Maybe it's time to throw out some good dares to your team to have them face something they view as scary or out of their comfort zone.

Try the following dares on your team:

- **Call on a prospect who is intimidating.**
  This prospect might have a string of initials at the end of his/her name or the deal size is twice your

average order. Dare your team to lay out a strategy for getting in front of this prospect. Dare them to get out of the comfort zone into the "sweat zone."

- **Invest money when you don't have the money.** The most successful reps I know don't wait for the company or someone else to make them successful. Dare your team to invest in activities that put them in front of ideal clients . . . *even if the company isn't buying.* That could mean attending a conference out of town, sponsoring an event, or buying a membership to an exclusive club.

- **Ask the tough questions during a sales call.** Prospects invest money with the sales professionals who are willing to run a "sixty minutes" sales call. Asking good, tough, critical questions sets you apart from the salesperson who still believes he/she can "nice" a prospect into giving them dollars and business. As a client of mine once said, "I will engage the salesperson who makes my brain hurt!"

- **Set a goal that scares you.**
  Have your sales team write down what they want to earn this year. Now, have your team double that number. Dare them to raise their own personal expectations of what they think they are worth. Remind them that they are the only ones setting their limits.

- **Ask for help.**
  Set the egos aside and ask for help in areas where they are not proficient. It might be time management, asking for referrals, or giving a sales presentation. Top producers ask for help so they are not helpless.

- **Lose their mediocre friends.**
  Remind your team that who they "hang" with in sales will insure their success or failure. Mediocre performers like to stick around other mediocre performers. The bar for success is low and membership criteria easy—expect and accept less.

The game of "Dare" isn't just for sales people. Sales managers also need to partake in the "Dare" game.

Just like your sales team, you may have areas that require you moving out of your comfort zone.

I dare you to:

- **Engage in tough love.**

  A great sales manager is similar to a great parent. Good parents set expectations of behavior and character for their children and hold their kids accountable to those expectations. I dare you to put aside the popularity contest and refuse to accept excuses or cave in when the sales team pushes back on standards of excellence. I dare you to put aside the need to be liked for the need to be respected. Tough love creates sustainable sales organizations, just like sustainable families.

- **Prospect for better prospects.**

  Sales managers must prospect; however, the target changes. Instead of prospecting for business, sales managers must be consistently prospecting for top sales talent. Take a look at who you are recruiting. Are you going after top producers or average producers because you believe your company is too small or not well branded enough to attract the best? I dare you to go after the best and use your selling skills to persuade them to join your team and the opportunities at your company.

- **Show more appreciation.**
  High-driving types often land in the position of sales manager because of their ability to achieve goals. High drivers, as a profile, don't need a lot of strokes and are very results-oriented. In fact, they even think that if they show too much appreciation, their sales team will quit working. I dare you to change your old (and outdated) style and start giving out more pats on the back, creating recognition programs and setting up events to hit the fun quota.

You are never too old to play "Dare." Create a daredevil sales culture by practicing one of my favorite quotes from Eleanor Roosevelt, "Do something that scares you everyday." Get scared and watch the growth!

Lesson 19

Count Your Blessings

It is time to close and the final chapter will be short. The shortness of the chapter does not reflect the content, for it is perhaps the most important content of the book: Creating a sales team that embraces a spirit of gratitude.

I was challenged in writing this chapter trying to think of a specific story that illustrates where I learned to be a person of gratitude. Maybe it evolved from starting every meal giving thanks for the food. Or perhaps it evolved from hearing both my parents say, during financially tough times, "If you have your health, you have everything." Whatever the source, I find it a great heartland principle that can serve us well in business.

I think it is easy for many of us in business to be grateful when things are going well but not so easy when "rain and hail" hit. Perhaps it is the perspective you give the adversity. Let's see if we can change the view.

- Be thankful when you have a "pit" at the bottom of your stomach during a sales call. It means you are showing up and trying—before you are good!

- Be thankful for the tough prospect. They make you appreciate your solid, repeat customers.

- Be thankful for good competition. They prevent you from becoming complacent.

- Be thankful for a tough boss. Their expectation of excellence helps you achieve your full potential.

- Be thankful for being tired at the end of a workday. Many unemployed would walk a mile in your shoes.

- Be thankful for failure. The lessons are priceless and only come with experience.

- Be thankful you live in a country where you can still "show up and try."

- Be thankful for the profession of sales. It is one of the few where you are still paid for your personal performance and perseverance.

I am thankful you chose to read this book. I hope the "lessons from the cornfield" serve you well in your sales leadership role.

How to Contact the Author

SalesLeadership, Inc.

cstanley@salesleadershipdevelopment.com

www.salesleadershipdevelopment.com

I am interested in:

☐ Learning more about workshops/keynotes/consulting offered by SalesLeadership

☐ Ordering SalesLeadership's Success Products (check out our store on the website)

- Prospecting . . . That Really Works
- Selecting and Hiring Top Sales Talent
- How To Get Paid What You Are Worth

Name: ______________________________

Company: ______________________________

Position: ______________________________

Address: ______________________________

City: ________________ State: _____ Zip: ______

Business Phone: ______________________________

A brief description of your company: ______________

____

____

____